The Poetry of Laurence Binyon

Volume XIV – The Secret: Sixty Poems

Robert Laurence Binyon, CH, was born on August 10th, 1869 in Lancaster in Lancashire, England to Quaker parents, Frederick Binyon and Mary Dockray.

He studied at St Paul's School, London before enrolling at Trinity College, Oxford, to read classics.

Binyon's first published work was Persephone in 1890. As a poet, his output was not prodigious and, in the main, the volumes he did publish were slim. But his reputation was of the highest order. When the Poet Laureate, Alfred Austin, died in 1913, Binyon was considered alongside Thomas Hardy and Rudyard Kipling for the post which was given to Robert Bridges.

Binyon played a pivotal role in helping to establish the modernist School of poetry and introduced imagist poets such as Ezra Pound, Richard Aldington and H.D. (Hilda Doolittle) to East Asian visual art and literature. Most of his career was spent at The British Museum where he produced many books particularly centering on the art of the Far East.

Moved and shaken by the onset of the World War I and its military tactics of young men slaughtered to hold or gain a few yards of shell-shocked mud Binyon wrote his seminal poem *For the Fallen*. It became an instant classic, turning moments of great loss into a National and human tribute.

After the war, he returned to the British Museum and wrote numerous books on art; especially on William Blake, Persian and Japanese art.

In 1931, his two volume Collected Poems appeared and in 1933, he retired from the British Museum.

Between 1933 and 1943, Binyon published his acclaimed translation of Dante's *Divine Comedy* in an English version of terza rima.

During the Second World War Binyon wrote another poetic masterpiece *'The Burning of the Leaves'*, about the London Blitz.

Robert Laurence Binyon died in Dunedin Nursing Home, Bath Road, Reading, on March 10th, 1943 after undergoing an operation.

Index of Contents

POEM I

THE SECRET

I

I lay upon my bed in the great night:
The sense of my body drowsed;
But a clearness yet lingered in the spirit,
By soft obscurity housed.

As an inn to a traveller on a long road,
Happy sleep appeared.
I should come there, to the room of waiting dreams,
In the time that slowly neared;

But still amid memory's wane fancy delighted,
Like wings in the afterglow
Dipping to the freshness of the waves of living,
To recover from long-ago

A touch or a voice, then soaring aloft and afar
The free world to range.
At last, on the brink of the dark, by subtle degrees
Came a chilling and a change.

Solitude sank to my marrow and pierced my veins.
Though I roam and though I learn
All the wonder of earth and of men, it is here
In the end I must return.

To the something alone that in each of us breathes and sleeps,
Profound, isolate, still,
And must brave the giant world, and from hour to hour
Must prove its own will;

To this self, unexcused and unglorified, drawn
From its fond shadows, and bare,

Wherein no man that has been, none that is or shall be.
Shares, or can ever share.

And it tingled through me how all use and disguise
Hide nothing: none
Avails to shield, neither pleader nor protector.
But the truth of myself alone.

And the days that have made me, have I not made them also?
Are they not drops of my blood?
What have I done with them? Flower they still within me.
Or lie, trodden in the mud?

Why for god-like freedom an irreplaceable Here,
An irrevocable Now?
They were heavy like strong chains about my bosom,
Like hard bonds upon my brow.

The moments oozing out of the silence seemed
From my very heart lost
In the stream of the worlds: I felt them hot like tears
And of more than riches' cost.

Yet what was it alien in me stood and rebelled
And cried, Nevertheless
My passion is mine, my strength and my frailty I am not
Thrall unto Time's duress!

Then suddenly rose before me, older than all,
Night of the soft speech.
With murmur of tender winds, yet terrible with stars
Beyond fancy's reach;

Without foundation, without summit, without
Haven or refuge, Night
Palpitating with stars that dizzy thought and desire
In their unimagined flight,

O these most terrible! vast surmises, touching
The pulse of a fear unknown.
Where all experience breaks like a frail bubble,
And the soul is left alone.

Alone and abandoned of all familiar uses, —
Itself the only place
It knows, — a question winged, barbed and burning
In the answerless frost of Space.

I was afraid; but my heart throbbed faster, fiercer.
I trembled, but cried anew:
I am strange to you, O Stars! O Night, I am your exile,
I have no portion in you.

Though you shall array your silences against me,
I know you and defy.
Though I be but a moth in an abyss of ages.
This at least is not yours; it is I.

II

O blessed be the touch of thought
That marries moments from afar.
That finds the thing it had not sought,
And smells a spice no treasure bought,
And learns what never sages taught.
And sees this earth a dazzling star!

As in the sheen of a lamp unseen,
The lamp of memory shrouded long.
There sprang before me, sweet as song,
The vision of a branch of bloom,
A swaying branch of blossom scented;
And in that bloom amid the gloom
My heart was luminously tented.

III

A score of years was melted, and I was young
And the world young with me.
When in innocence of delight I laid me down
Beneath a certain tree.

The breathing splendour of that remembered May
Had yet seven days to spill
In fragrant showers of fairy white and red
And in notes from the blackbird's bill,

When I laid me down on a bank by the water's edge:
In the glowing shadow I lay.
My very body was drenched in a speechless joy
Whose cause I could not say.

The sky was poured in singing rivers of blue;
The ripple danced in sight;

Close to the marge was a coloured pebble; it burned
Amid kisses of liquid light.

Like a hurry of little flames the tremble of gleams
Shivered up through the leaves and was gone.
Like a shaking of heavenly bells was the sound of the leaves
In the tower of branches blown.

And odours wandering each from its honeyed haunt
Over the air stole,
Like memories out of a world before the world,
Seeking the private soul.

But I knew not where my soul was: in that hour
Neither time nor place it knew!
It was trembling high in the topmost blossom that drank
Of the glory of airy blue;

It was dark in the root that sucked of the plenteous earth;
It was lovely flames of fire;
It was water that murmured round and around the world;
It was poured in the sun's desire.

Not the bird, but the bird's bright, wayward swiftness;
Not the flowers in magic throng.
But the shooting, the breathing and the perfumed breaking;
Not the singer it was, but the song.

I touched the flesh of my body, and it was strange.
It seemed that my spirit knew
It was I no more; yet the earth and the sky answered
And cried aloud. It is you!

Then into my blood the word of my being thrilled,
(Not a nerve but aware) — It is I!
Yet I could not tell my thought from the green of the grass.
My bliss from the blue of the sky.

Overbrimmed, overflowing, I rose like one who has drunk
Of a radiance keener than wine.
I stood on the marvellous earth, and felt my blood
As the stream of a power divine.

Laughter of children afar on the air came to me
And touched me softly home.
There were tears in me like trembling dew; I knew not
Where they had stolen from.

Who is not my brother, and who is not my sister?
O wonder of human eyes.
Have I passed you by, nor perceived how luminous in you
All infinity lies?

Love opened my eyes and opened my ears; not one.
But his soul is as mine is to me!
I heard like a ripple around the world breaking
The voices of children in glee;

I saw the beauty, secret as starlit wells,
Treasured in the bosoms of the old.
I heard like the whisper of leaf to leaf in the night-wind
Hopes that the tongue never told.

Was it the grass that quivered about me? I felt
Not that, but the hearts beating
Close to my own, unnumbered as blades of the grass,
And the dead in the quick heart meeting;

And I knew the dreams of wandering sorrow and joy
Breathed in the sleep of the night
From the other side of the earth, that for me was glowing
To the round horizon's light;

The earth that moves through the light and the dark for ever,
As a dancer moves among
The maze of her sister stars, with a silent speed
In a dance that is always young:

And the heart of my body knew that it shared in all;
It was there, not alone nor afraid.
It throbbed in the life that can never be destroyed.
In the things Time never made.

POEM II

For Mercy, Courage, Kindness, Mirth,
There is no measure upon earth.
Nay, they wither, root and stem.
If an end be set to them.

Overbrim and overflow
If your own heart you would know.
For the spirit, born to bless.
Lives but in its own excess.

POEM III

Naked night; black elms, pallid and streaming sky!
Alone with the passion of the Wind,
In a hollow of stormy sound lost and alone am I,
On beaten earth a lost, unmated mind,
Marvelling at the stars, few, strange, and bright.
That all this dark assault of surging air,
Wrenching the rooted wood, hunting the cloud of night,
As if it would tear all and nothing spare,
Leaves supreme in the height.

Against what laws, what laws, what powers invisible.
Unsought yet always found.
Cries this dumb passion, strains this wrestle of wild will.
With tiger-leaps that seem to shake the ground?
Is it the baffled, homeless, rebel wind's crying
Or storm from a profounder passion wrung?
Ah, heart of man, is it you, the old powers defying,

By far desires and terrible beauty stung.
Broken on laws unseen, in a starry world dying
Ignorant, tameless, young?

POEM IV

SURRENDER

Pale was the early day.
Fog-white the winter air,
When up a hill-side bare,
Roughened with rimy grass,
I took my thoughtless way.

As my feet strayed uphill
I felt the blank cloud float
Past, and bedew my coat.
At unawares I found
A gate, and there stood still.

And on a sudden behold,
Above, the virgin blue.
Blue, bathing my heart through!

A shock of blueness bright
Pierced with an eye of gold.

And there uprising tall
From mist to warm sapphire,
Straight up like windless fire,
A poplar stood alone.
White, dream-fresh, virginal.

Rime robed her, pure as snow.
white was never white
As this which thrilled my sight.
I stood still in the mist,
Dazzled, entranced, aglow.

For in a dazzling drift
The rime rained down, it gleamed,
It shivered soft, it streamed,
Radiant as tears of joy
When the heart gives all its gift.

Alone in the still, still air
To the divine lone height
Of blue this poplar white
Like virgin ecstasy
Stript all her beauty bare.

POEM V

Nothing is enough!
No, though our all be spent-
Heart's extremest love,
Spirit's whole intent,
All that nerve can feel,
All that brain invent, —
Still beyond appeal
Will Divine Desire
Yet more excellent
Precious cost require
Of this mortal stuff, —
Never be content
Till ourselves be fire.
Nothing is enough!

I think of a flower that no eye ever has seen,
That springs in a solitary air.
Is it no one's joy? It is beautiful as a queen
Without a kingdom's care.

We have built houses for Beauty, and costly shrines.
And a throne in all men's view:
But she was far on a hill where the morning shines
And her steps were lost in the dew.

PAIN

Find me out a fortress, find
Such a mind within the mind
As can gather to its source
All of life's inveterate force,
Find the hard and secret cell
In my body's citadel,
Iron-ribbed from suck and drain
Of the clutching monster, Pain —
Pain, the formless alien will
That seeks me out, that strives to drill
Through shielding thought and barricade
Of all the strength my will has made;
That singles me and searches through
The sharp sense I am narrowed to;
And ever as the bond I strain
Thrusts me home to flesh again,
Estranging me from earth, to be
One fierce throb of identity!
Yet there's fibre in the mind
I shall find, I shall find.
To resist and to defy
All the world that is not I.

Trees are for lovers.
A spirit has led them
Where the young boughs meet

And the green light hovers.
And shadowy winds blow sweet.
Trees spring to heaven!
So their hearts would spring,
So would they outpour
All the heart discovers
Of its own wild treasure
Into speech, and sing
Like the tree from its core
Sweet words beyond measure
Like leaves in the sun
Dancing every one
And weaving a fairy
Cave of quivering rays
And of shadows starry
Where those lovers, drowned
Each in the other's gaze.
Lose all time, abound
In their perfect giving;
Give and never tire
Of their fulness, still
In the fresh leaves living
One full song unsated
Of the flower Desire
And Delight the fruit;
Love, that's mated.

POEM IX

THE MEETING

Faces of blank decorum, and bald heads
And the drone of a voice saying what none denies;

Words like cobwebs, scarcely stirred by a breath,
Loosely hanging, grey in an unswept corner,

Thoughts belonging to nobod3^ like old coats
Cheaply borrowed out of a dead man's wardrobe.

Over his spectacles looks the Chairman, blandly
Solemn, exacting attention, nodding approval.

I look on the floor and ponder the shaven planks, —
Tall trees once, tossing aloft in the wild air;

I watch the sun that falls upon oaken carvings,
A gentle beam from millions of miles away:

Hands and a chisel carved them, — at night the lips
Of the carver blew the dust from his work and smiled.

The chairs, so silent under the ponderous flesh, —
Pleasure shaped them out of a brain's designing.

The brass of the chandelier, the molten metal
Streamed in the mould, conspired to friendly uses.

I feel the spring of the trees and their old rejoicing.
The touch of the warmth of hands that felt for beauty.

Near and neighbourly are those shapes about me.
Taking the light sweetly and saying nothing.

Why is a voice, the only human assertion.
Farther away than the suns of the astronomers?

POEM X

From the howl of the wind
As I opened the door
And entered, the firelight
Was soft on the floor.

Mute each in their places
Were table and chair.
The white wall, the shadows,
Awaiting me there.

All was strange on a sudden!
From the stillness a spell,
A fear or a fancy,
Across my heart fell.

Were they waiting another
To sit by the hearth?
Was it I saw them newly,
A stranger on earth?

POEM XI

THE AUGUST WEEDS

I wandered between woods
On a grassy down, when still
Clouds hung after rain
Over hollow and hill;

The blossom-time was over.
The singing throats dumb.
And the year's coloured ripeness
Not yet come.

And all at unawares.
Surprising the stray sight.
Ran straight into my heart
Like a beam, delight.

Negligent weeds ravelled
The green edge of the copse,
Whitely, dimly, sparkling
With a million drops.

And sudden fancy feigned
What strange beauty would pass
Did but a shiver of wind
Tremble through the grass,

Shaking the poised, round drops
Spilled and softly rolled
A-glitter from the ragwort's
Roughened gold;

From the rusted scarlet
Of tall sorrel seed.
And fretted tufts, frost-grey.
Of the silver-weed.

And from purple-downed thistle
Towering dewy over
Yellow-cupped spurge
And the drenched, sweet clover.

But all were motionless:
Not one breath shed
Those little pale pearls
That an elf might thread

Under a fading moon
By an old thorn-tree
For the witching throat
Of Nimuè.

POEM XII

Thinking of shores that I shall never see,
And things that I would know but am forbid
By Time and briefness, treasuries locked from me
In unknown tongue or human bosom hid.

Knowing how unsure is all my knowledge, doled
To sloven memory and to cheated sense,
And to what majesty of stars I hold
My little candle of experience

In the vast night, in the untravelled night,
I sigh and seek. And there is answer none
But in the silence that sure pressure slight
Of your heart beating close beside my own.

O Love, Love, where in you is any bound?
Fool I to seek, who have infinitely found.

POEM XIII

The rain was ending, and light
Lifting the leaden skies.
It shone upon ceiling and floor
And dazzled a child's eyes.

Pale after fever, a captive
Apart from his schoolfellows.
He stood at the high room's window
With face to the pane pressed close.

And beheld an immense glory
Flooding with fire the drops
Spilled on miraculous leaves
Of the fresh green lime-tree tops.

Washed gravel glittered red
To a wall, and beyond it nine

Tall limes in the old inn yard
Rose over the tall inn sign.

And voices arose from beneath
Of boys from school set free,
Racing and chasing each other
With laughter and games and glee.

To the boy at the high room-window.
Gazing alone and apart,
There came a wish without reason,
A thought that shone through his heart.

I'll choose this moment and keep it,
He said to himself, for a vow.
To remember for ever and ever
As if it were always now.

POEM XIV

Angered Reason walked with me
A street so squat, unshapen, bald.
So blear-windowed and grimy-walled,
So dismal-doored, it seemed to be

The abortion of a mind that had
Nor wit nor will to make, but left
Its impotence in image, reft
Of even the means of seeming glad.

And there, like never-ripened fruit,
Unsunned and starved, were human lives
In joyless, neighbour-dreading hives
Of care, with half their senses mute.

It pressed on me, that patient street.
It hurt me that it housed my kind:
It was so abject and resigned
And so deformed, I hated it.

The stars that flowered above grew bright;
The evening filled with wondrous blue;
The lampshine glistened in the dew;
The gliding trams were ships of light.

And through my rebel heart there ran

The want of things not bought or sold;
The spirit free to make and mould;
The naked glory of a man.

And fevered I began to build
A city, like the body, worth
The natural happiness of earth,
And with this folk its streets I filled,

No more from widest joy exiled
Nor helpless in a caging net.
Suddenly by a lamp I met
A woman carrying her child.

I stopped the building of my dream:
For there was all the future's book
Written in that enfolding look,
And there the never-ending theme,

And there the builder of the strong
City of men's desire; but there
Also the shadow of the snare
And the corruption and the wrong.

Ah, now I doubted of my thought
That could so easily perfect
Wishes in dream, and raise the wrecked.
And make all noble as it wrought.

Those mother's eyes, absorbed, unknown,
Had made my vision wan and thin.
There was a harder world to win
From flesh and blood than wood and stone.

O now of those, life's prisoners, none.
Soiled, soured, or hardened, but had speech
To me of secret wonder; each
Was once so wonderful to one!

Yet she that bears the pang, and hears
The first young cry and stills its want,
And can with her vast hope enchant
The promise of betraying years, —

Who should have beauty's best but she
To whom a son is given? That street
Of life's denial and defeat
Stood in my mind, accusing me.

THE THINGS THAT GROW

It was nothing but a little neglected garden,
Laurel-screened, and hushed in a hot stillness;
An old pear-tree, and flowers mingled with weeds.
Yet as I came to it all unawares, it seemed
Charged with mystery; and I stopped, intruding.
Fearful of hurting that so absorbed stillness.
For I was tingling with the wind's salty splendour,
And still my senses moved with the keel's buoyance
Out on the water, where strong light was shivered
Into a dance dazzling as drops of flame.
The rocking radiance and the winged sail's lifting
And the noise of the rush of the water left behind
Sang to my body of movement, victory, joy.
But here the light was asleep, and green, green
In a veined leaf it glowed among the shadows.
A hollyhock rose to the sun and bathed its flowers
Luminously clustered in the unmoving air;
A butterfly lazily winked its gorgeous wings;
Marigolds burned intently amid the grass;
The ripening pears hung each with a rounded shadow:
All beyond was drowned in the indolent blueness.
And at my feet, like a word of an unknown tongue.
Was the midnight-dark bloom of the delicate pansy.
Suddenly these things awed my heart, as if here
In perishing blossom and springing shoot were a power
Greater than shipwrecking winds and all wild waters.

POEM XVI

The night wind over the great downs
Streams along the sky.
In the solitude of the hill-side
There is only you and I.

The night wind leaps and rushes
Black in the trees that cry
As if their travail echoed
The world's eternal why?

Clouds have buried the old moon.
The sunk light cowers shy.
In a world of stumbling and darkness
There is only you and I.

I am weary of doing and dating
The day with the thing to be done,
This painful self translating
To a language not my own.

Give me to fashion a thing;
Give me to shape and to mould;
I have found out the song I can sing,
I am happy, delivered, and bold.

THE BATHER

Water, frolic water!
Drops in the dazzle of noon, drops divinely cold,
Radiant down naked breast, down arm and thigh
You run to my feet, shaken to shining grass.
Betwixt the green blades, liquid gems, you lie.
Water, careless water!
Little miraculous mirrors
Globing the glory of earth and sky,
Lazy drops, vanishing in the sun's hot kisses.
Drops caressingly rolled,
You glide and suddenly fall like a falling star.
Like a throb of delight you die.
The pool beneath me glows
In its own gloom asleep,
Water, secret water!
But all its quivering sparkles, a fairy mesh.
Are showered about my sun-delighted flesh.
And I wonder at the beauty of water.
Simple and swift and shy,
A slumber and escape.
Any whither yielding,
A never-recovered shape.
Laughter and loss in an instant's gleam to the eye!

Water, vivid water!
I feel the cool drops run
Down me in the sun;
And suddenly thrilling near
In the stillness of noon is a vision of water swung
In waves heavy and huge
Out of a chaos shaped into shapes of fear
Heedless of human cry,
Drowning, ruining, endlessly crashed and returning,—
A power, a terror! O cold, dancing drops,
Is it the kiss of a danger in delight
That makes you glow on the body of a man
And the heart of a man reply?

POEM XIX

In the shadow of a broken house,
Down a deserted street,
Propt walls, cold hearths, and phantom stairs,
And the silence of dead feet —
Locked wildly in one another's arms
I saw two lovers meet.

And over that hearthless house aghast
Rose from the mind's abyss
Lost stars and ruined, peering moons,
Worlds overshadowing this, —
Time's stony palace crumbled down
Before that instant kiss.

POEM XX

Where do you float from, visions that shine ere sleep
Subdues with leaden law
The dancing fires of the brain? — In a shadowy land.
As a king from a tower I saw.

There came startled gazelles, beautifully leaping,
Delicate-hoofed: they were gone.
And the red pomegranate showered its petalled bloom
On the glittering stream alone.

I saw the dust on an Indian plain, and a grove
Where pilgrims went in white:

I saw the mountains, throned upon purple air.
Remote in sculptured light.

And I saw the broadening beams of the early sun
On the pale Pacific melt.
And naked fishermen, idly rocked in a boat;
Their briny nets I smelt.

I saw amid Asian deserts a bed of reeds,
And a heron slowly rose
To the cloud from wild reeds blown by a wind that came
From a land no man yet knows.

And I watched a tall ship gliding out of the mist
By a snow-seamed iron cape.
The smoky wraiths clung round her, but on she stemmed.
Self-willed, a wing-bright shape.

Then all fell dark. Yet still in a trance elate.
And strange to myself I lay.
Here was the black, soft stillness: but where was I?
Far away, far away.

POEM XXI

NUMBERS

Trefoil and Quatrefoil!
What shaped those destinied small silent leaves
Or numbered them under the soil?
I lift my dazzled sight
From grass to sky,
From humming and hot perfume
To scorching, quivering light, —
Empty blue! — Why,
As I bury my face afresh
In a sunshot vivid gloom —
Minute infinity's mesh.
Where spearing side by side
Smooth stalk and furred uplift
Their luminous green secrets from the grass,
Tower to a bud and delicately divide —
Do I think of the things unthought
Before man was?

Bodiless Numbers!

When there was none to explore
Your winding labyrinths occult,
None to delve your ore
Of strange virtue, or do
Your magical business, you
Were there, never old nor new,
Veined in the world and alive:
Before the planets. Seven;
Before these fingers, Five!

You that are globed and single,
Crystal virgins, and you that part,
Melt, and again mingle!
We have hoisted sail in the night
On the oceans that you chart:
Dark winds carry us onward, on;
But you are there before us, silent Answers,
Beyond the bounds of the sun.
You body yourselves in the stars, inscrutable dancers.
Native where we are none.

O inhuman Numbers!
All things change and glide.
Corrupt and crumble, suffer wreck and decay,
But, obstinate dark Integrities, you abide.
And obey but them who obey.
All things else are dyed
In the colours of man's desire:
But you no bribe nor prayer
Avails to soften or sway.
Nothing of me you share,
Yet I cannot think you away.
And if I seek to escape you, still you are there,
Stronger than caging pillars of iron.
Not to be passed, in an air
Where human wish and word
Fall like a frozen bird.

Music asleep
In pulses of sound, in the waves!
Hidden runes rubbed bright!
Dizzy ladders of thought in the night!
Are you masters or slaves —
Subtlest of man's slaves —
Shadowy Numbers?

In a vision I saw
Old vulture Time, feeding

On the flesh of the world; I saw
The home of our use outdated —
Seasons of fruiting and seeding
Withered, and hunger and thirst
Dead, with all they fed on:
Till at last, when Time was sated,
Only you persisted,
Daedal Numbers, sole and same,
Invisible skeleton frame
Of the peopled earth we tread on —
Last, as first.

Because naught can avail
To wound or to tarnish you;
Because you are neither sold nor bought,
Because you have not the power to fail
But live beyond our furthest thought,
Strange Numbers, of infinite clue.
Beyond fear, beyond ruth.
You strengthen also me
To be in my own truth.

POEM XXII

THE TWO DESIRES

What is the spirit's desire.
Sprung, springing, singing,
Fountain-fresh, rainbowed over with lights that awaken
The inner dishevelled crystal, starrily shaken
To sevenfold changes of fire?

Youth in its wonder aflower,
Up to the sun swinging,
A March daffodil, braves the bright wind's cold —
Sensitive silken softness, yet how bold
Against the cold snow-flurry and sleet shower!
Because it seeks — what mark
Beyond the tower of the lark
Who sees the dawn from the dark?
Only itself to unfold,
Expand, outpour, be told,
All, all to utter, —
Delicate thought's moth-flutter,
And hope's proud-sweeping voyage of wings sky-reaping;
To soar and to explore

In the midst of this mind-soiling
Earth-medley, and flesh- toiling
Cares, betrayal, and pain's returning sting;
Still to spring, still to sing,
Flame and flower of the mind.
Seeking bliss in this, —
Itself, itself to find.

What is the spirit's desire?
— Comes Experience after.
Experience and Comparison, mockers old.
Trail of a tarnishing cloud is heavily rolled.
And, harsher than shadow or cold.
Pitiless light searches the shallows of laughter
For terrible truth in the world rock-seated.
Yet not because shadow-fearing or world-defeated
But natively in its own unprompted sort.
Because of desire profounder than desire,
O now where aims the spirit? Higher, higher

Than ever flight up-carried it! Now that aim
Is a greatness greater than hero's name and fame,
A beauty passionate more than flesh can support,
Divine greatness, divine beauty, a pain
Appeasing all pains; flying not blight or bruise,
But seeking its own afar-conceived resort.
The spirit is only fain
Itself to lose,
Lose, lose.

POEM XXIII

In the high leaves of a walnut.
On the very topmost boughs,
A boy that climbed the branching bole
His cradled limbs would house.

On the airy bed that rocked him
Long, idle hours he'd lie
Alone with white clouds sailing
The warm blue of the sky.

I remember not what his dreams were;
But the scent of a leaf's enough
To house me higher than those high boughs
In a youth he knew not of.

In a light that no day brings now
But none can spoil or smutch,
A magic that I felt not then
And only now I touch.

COMMERCIAL

Gross, with protruding ears,
Sleek hair, brisk glance, fleshy and yet alert.
Red, full, and satisfied.
Cased in obtuseness confident not to be hurt.

He sits at a little table
In the crowded, congenial glare and noise, jingling
Coins in his pocket; sips
His glass, with hard eye impudently singling

A woman here and there: —
Women and men, they are all priced in his thought,
All commodities staked
In the market, sooner or later sold and bought.

"Were I he," you are thinking.
You with the dreamer's forehead and pure eyes,
"What should I lose?—All,
All that is worth the striving for, all my prize;

"All the truth of me, all
Life that is wonder, pity and fear, requiring
Utter joy, utter pain.
From the heart that the infinite hurts with deep desiring.

"Why is it I am not he?
Chance? The grace of God? The mystery's plan?
He, too, is human stuff,
A kneading of the old, brotherly slime of man.

"Am I a lover of men.
And turn abhorring as from fat slug or snake?
Lives obstinate in me too
Something the power of angels could not unmake?"

O self-questioner! None

Unlocks your answer. Steadily look, nor flinch.
This belongs to your kind.
And knows its aim, and fails not itself at a pinch.

It is here in the world and works,
Not done with yet. — Up, then, let the test be tried!
Dare your uttermost, be
Completely, and of your own, like him, be justified.

POEM XXV

THE TAMARISK HEDGE

I know that there are slumbrous woods beyond
On islands of white marges, where the tide
Floods upward, blue as a kingfisher's wing.
And sails, like wishes of a reverie,
Shine to the wind that fills them, far inland.
I know that there are harbours in the hills
Amid those verdurous, smooth bosom-folds.
Found by the idle sunbeams for their sleep.
But it contents me to see nothing more
Than liquid blue of the invisible wind
Flowing and glowing through the tamarisk
That waves upon this wild deserted bank;
And I lie warm on the short, sandy turf
Lulled in bright noise of the returning sea.
O plumy Tamarisk, tossing your green hair
In the wind's radiant stream, as if I had lent
Your fibres all my senses of delight.
Why does it so enchant me to have nothing.
And drink long draughts ot sky where nothing is,
And tremble to the glory of an hour
That passes out of nothing into nothing?

POEM XXVI

Shabby house-wall
Of bricks once yellow,
Dingied with city grime.
Dusty and sallow,

The High sun, glorying
In clear gold, edges

Your crumbled mortar's
Luminous ledges.

You glow with a touch
From the pure sky.
And suddenly all
Is new to the eye.

I see you as labour's
Rough fruit and homely,
Raised morning by morning
To an order comely;

Labour of hands long dead.
Living, when all's at rest.
After the dark has come
And the light gone West.

POEM XXVII

What is lovelier than rain that lingers
Falling through the western light?
The light that's red between my fingers
Bathes infinite heaven's remotest height.

Whither will the cloud its darkness carry
Whose trembling drops about me spill?
Two worlds, of shadow and splendour, marry
I stand between them rapt and still.

POEM XXVIII

Drinking wide, sunny wind.
Hand wathin hand.
We look from hill to hill
Of our own land.

Hand within hand, we remember
Without speech,
And hour upon hour comes about us
We number them each.

O little far clouds that swim
In the round of blue,

Are you bringing those hours again,
Shining in you?

You melt into air, drop on earth,
Sucked up in the light.
And again you appear, in the blue
You are born, you are bright,

As those hours live in us, nay beyond;
When we die, they shall still
Lift our hearts up, as now we uplift
Our hearts on the hill.

POEM XXIX

THE HOUSE THAT WAS

Of the old house, only a few, crumbled
Courses of brick, smothered in nettle and dock,
Or a shaped stone lying mossy where it tumbled!
Sprawling bramble and saucy thistle mock
What once was fire-lit floor and private charm,
Whence, seen in a windowed picture, were hills fading
At night, and all was memory-coloured and warm,
And voices talked, secure of the wind's invading.

Of the old garden, only a stray shining
Of daffodil flames among April's cuckoo-flowers
Or clustered aconite, mixt with weeds entwining!
But, dark and lofty, a royal cedar towers
By homelier thorns; and whether the rain drifts
Or sun scorches, he holds the downs in ken.
The western vales; his branchy tiers he lifts,
Older than many a generation of men.

POEM XXX

Out of first sleep as they awoke
The moon had stolen upon her face.
It seemed that they had opened eyes
New on another world and place.

The eyes of each the other sought
Wondering; no sound was in the night.

On them the very soul of peace
Gazed in that spiritual light.

Beyond the reign of hurt and pain,
Beyond the boundaries of death,
Each seemed with their awaking sighs
To breathe at last their native breath.

FLAME AND SNOW

He bare branches rose against the grey sky.
Under them, freshly fallen, snow shone to the eye.

Up the hill-slope, over the brow it shone,
Spreading an immaterial beauty to tread upon.

In the elbow of black boughs it clung, nested white.
And smooth below it slept in the solitude of its light.

It was deep to the knee in the hollow; there in a stump of wood
I struck my bill-hook, warm to the fingers' blood, and stood,

Pausing, and breathed and listened: all the air around
Was filled with busy strokes and ringing of clean sound,

And now and again a crack and a slow rending, to tell
When a tree heavily tottered and swift with a crash fell.

I smelt the woody smell of smoke from the fire, now
Beginning to spurt from frayed bracken and torn bough

In the lee of a drift, fed from our long morning toil
And sending smart to the eyes the smoke in a blue coil.

I lopped the twigs from a fresh-cut pole and tossed it aside
To the stakes heaped beyond me, and made a plunging stride,

And gathered twines of bramble and dead hazel sticks
And a faggot of twisted thorn with snow lumped in the pricks,

And piled the smoulder high. Soon a blaze tore
Up through hissing boughs and shrivelling leaves, from a core

Of quivering crimson; soon the heat burst and revelled.

And apparitions of little airy flames dishevelled

Gleamed and vanished, a lost flight as of elfin wings,
Trembling aloft to the wild music that Fire sings

Dancing alive from nothing, lovely and mad. And still
The snow, pale as a dream, slept on the old hill.

Softly fallen and strange. Which made me more to glow.
Beauty of young flames, or wonder of young snow?

POEM XXXII

COMPANIONS

The bread that's broken when we eat together
Tastes sweet. A sunbeam stealing to your hand
Seems as if spilled from something brimming over
Within me, wanting no word, or itself
The word I wanted! Find we not our own
Language in winds, fresh from a golden place.
When breasting the high down at last we turn
To each other, bright with rapturous escape.
And the hills sing together, like our hearts.
Lost in the light! Between us, as we walk
Green roadsides, under homely hedgerow elms
Of summer leaf, silences are as water
Smooth for the sail and shining to the verge.
But intimate as a hand's touch when we pace
Long crowded pavements amber-lamped in dusk
That holds its dark breath over the gay talk,
Bright eyes, and grief buried in moving sound.
There is a secret colour that has dyed
The world within our hearts: none knows it else,
No more than that which thickens the flushed light
Deep in the foxglove's honey-throat; it is there
In the midst of light speech and forgetfulness,
In the empty house of absence, where the walls
Echo other voices; it is in the midst
Of the unsaid fears the mind plots forts against,
In the dragging thought and drizzle of blank care.
The daily doing of what must be done;
Then suddenly it glows and bathes us like the sun.

POEM XXXIII

We have planted a tree.
And behold, it has flowers.
How lovely their joy!
Yet they know not of ours.

Who have shared in dull cares
And the sharpness of pain
Yet feel in our kisses
The first kiss again.

And with hand clasped in hand
We turn and we see
The sweet laughing flowers
On our own fair tree.

POEM XXXIV

Pride is the untrue mask,
Shame is a cloak that clings.
Tenderness oft is a trammelling veil
Because of truth that stings.

O to be stript, and to use
All one's soul entire!
To be seen in the light, to be known for one's own,
To abound in the beauty of desire!

As the young man casts his clothes,
And, freed to the living air.
Runs down the radiant ocean-sands
With singing body bare.

POEM XXXV

Lose me, full, full moment,
Like a ripple round.
Widening into worlds
Beyond earth's bound.

I was walking a grey road
Dulled to an old aim:
Now I seek nothing,

Now I have no name.

How came you to me.
Opening timeless skies
Like a heaven within me
That is all sunrise?

Silences in the mind, the haunting Silences,
Silences daunting.
Chill as a cavern's air, immuring hollow gloom
Yet inly luring
Like springs that ooze there, glidings from the stone
What strange, dark tidings
You brim with! First, the doubted certainties.
Then fancies routed
By a spectral whisper from unstable worlds
That turns to fable
Accepted hope and fever of desires;
A whispered Never,
Out of a vapour clothing from afar
All things in Nothing.

THE THISTLE

In a patch of baked earth
At the crumbled cliff's brink,
Where the parching of August
Has cracked a long chink.

Against the blue void
Of still sea and sky
Stands single a thistle.
Tall, tarnished, and dry.

Frayed leaves, spotted brown.
Head hoary and torn.
Was ever a weed
Upon earth so forlorn,

So solemnly gazed on

By the sun in his sheen
That prints in long shadow
Its raggedness lean?

From the sky comes no laughter.
From earth not a moan.
Erect stands the thistle,
Its seeds abroad blown.

POEM XXXVIII

My boat swings out and back,
Moored among mint and rush.
The river's ruffled speed
Laughs in the white wind's track.
My idle fingers crush
A crinkled, scented reed.

Who needs his fate provoke?
A spirit in all things flows.
And I with them flow too,
Content to eye long boughs
Of silvering willow stroke
Slowly the summer blue.

POEM XXXIX

The long road lures across the hill.
Divides the brown fields and the green.
And curves, and dips, and climbing still
Gleams over into lands unseen.

I think what valleys far more fair
Than ours, the road runs on to meet.
The light falls wild and happy there.
What shadowy doubt delays my feet?

Oh, one day, one day, I shall go
Whither the road runs out of sight,
And find, whatever winds may blow.
An inn at falling of the night.

Round apples, burning upon the apple boughs.
As the evening flush withdraws.
Perfect and satiate, earth's completed vows,
In a stillness nothing flaws.

You burn in the branching golden green, you float
In humid blue immersed.
Strange as if gleaming out of an air remote
Where unknown tongues conversed.

Coloured and orbed by the hours, in motionless poise.
You are timed, and rounded, and still:
But in me is the want that springs, creates, destroys.
The want no hours fulfil.

Stirred but a wing, stole but a tremor of light
From the cloud, and my heart were aware
That its will is to be with the spirit whose joy is flight;
I have tasted a timeless air.

Spiritual laughter promises all things free,
The heart has a heaven to spend.
Where the mind imagines its own, perfection to me
Is a prison, a date, and an end.

POEM XLI

Time buys no wisdom like the eyes of youth,
Though youth itself be blinded with delight,
As a buoyant swimmer by the bursting spray
Of the resplendent surge, and know not yet
The marvel of its own heart's vision, blurred
By lovely follies dancing in the sun.
I heard a skylark scaling the spring air
As slow I climbed the misty, rough hill-side.
He poured the wordless wonder of his joy
Into the empty sky: was never word
Of human language held a joy so pure;
But it was I who knew it! Though my feet
Stayed on the plodded earth and in the mist.
Yet I could breathe, float, mount and sing with him,
The unweariable singer; I could bathe
In the beyond of blue, and know the round
Of sea beneath me, and the sun above.

He gave of what he knew not, soaring throat!

POEM XLII

HOLIDAY

Through Ebblesborne and Broad-Chalke
The narrow river runs,
Dimples with dark November rains,
Flashes in April suns.

But give me days of rosy June
And on warm grass to lie
And watch, bright over long green weed,
Quick water wimple by.

Blue swallows, arrowing up and down,
Cool trout that glide and dart.
Lend me their happy bodies
For the fancies of my heart.

But you, clear stream, that murmur
One music all day long,
I wish my idle fancy
Sang half so sweet a song.

POEM XLIII

ADVERSARIES

Who are these that meet
At random in the street?
Adversaries! Yet they
Make no sign nor stay.
Neither he nor she
Knows what those Powers be
That bodied in them go
Among the peopled flow,
One toward the dusk and one
Toward the Western sun.

Secret eyes turn to her,
And bosoms throb astir.
As if a perfume blew

And made the evening new.
Lissom with budding breast,
She steps toward the bright West,
An airy-footed shape!
Above the neck's young nape
Springs wonderful her hair.
The round throat lifts in air
The flower that is her head.
Her lips are Peril's red;
Her eyes a shy surprise,
Shedding soft cruelties.

Of what will was she wrought.
Vivid, without a thought?
Fragrance of all that's young
And delicately sprung
Is round her like a lure
Voluptuously pure; —
Eternal soul of sense,
The moment's quintessence!
Of what will was she made.
With those fine lashes laid
Upon her bloom? She comes
From the wild Earth, that hums
With summer in the mead,
Skitting the flower-cups' greed
Of sunlight; ill to tame
As Hunger, Thirst, or Flame.

But he that's striding East
Regards not her the least.
His thought is far away,
Circling the end of day.
Though young, the restless mind,
Moulding the flesh, has signed
His features; and his gaze.
Absented in retreat
From all this human street,
Holds musings that begin
To sharpen cheek and chin.
What speculation now
Beneath that ardent brow
Braves what it sees? — Among
Blind worlds, this planet swung
Like an old toy, a spark
In the gigantic dark,
A mote of dust alive.
Where millions meanly strive—

For what?

If Thought alone
Keeps man upon his throne
Of courage, to outface
The Gorgon mask of Space,
What wills it with this house
Of flesh, that loves to drowse
And take the hours of sense
For sweetness and defence, —
Of flesh that is but clay
For Thought to sift away
Like powder of idle sand
Within the crumbling hand?

Two Cruelties are these,
And two Defiances.
Yet though they be apart
As East and West, the heart
Of man is twined in each.
Of them he makes his speech.
His torment and delight.
His songs, his tears, his height
Of wisdom, his despair.
Though both his being tear.
He knows not which to choose
Nor which he'd harder lose.

POEM XLIV

THE SEVEN ISLES

I dream of western waters, and of the Seven Isles,
And of mornings when they appear
Flowering out of the mist on a sea of smiles.
Warm and familiar and near.

Then O how changed! fugitive, faint, remote;
In another world than ours.
Vanishing apparitions, they seemed to float;
Shadows of shadowy powers.

Effaced, at last, as if they had never been!
Drowned in the empty bay.
On solitary water was nothing to be seen
But a sail, pale on the grey.

And I wonder, O Isles, reappearing and lost without sign
In the solitude of the seas.
Are the songs of the Immortals more divine
Or their magical silences?

If I could sing the song of her
Who makes my heart to sing;
If I could catch the words to match
Its secret blossoming;

My song should be a heaven of sound
Thrilled through a single note, —
The world of light that's infinite
In one flower's honey-throat!

A fountain diamonded in air.
Earth-blessing dews at night,
A dancing child, flames lovely-wild,
Should not so much delight.

But where I most have theme to boast
I stammer in my speech;
The full heart shames my faltering art
With music past its reach.

THE CATHEDRAL PORCH

Towering, towering up to the noon-blaze.
Up to the hot blue, up to blinding gold,
Pillar and pinnacle, arch and corbel, scrolled.
Flowered and tendrilled, soar, aspire and raise
The giant porch, with kings and prophets old
High in their niches, like one shout of praise.
From earth to heaven. — In shadow of the door
Cringing, a beggar stands;
He holds out abject hands;
His lips for pity and alms mechanically implore.

Splendour of air and the bright splintered beam

Carve all afresh in strong reverberate glow
As if even now the passionate master-blow
Struck from the stone the shapes of beauty's dream.
Can a mere hand ever have fashioned so
Desire's adventure, god-like force, supreme
Sky-scaling joy? — The beggar's toneless drone
Comes from his laughterless
Accepted wretchedness
As from a long-dried well, where off-cast clutter's thrown.

Prophet and saint and kingly king, whose eyes.
Flashing authority, gaze and awe, you came
From wombs of flesh, though now enthroned in fame.
A mother heard the helpless wailing cries
Of voices that have won the world's acclaim
By wisdom, suffering, truth. August you rise
Above this wreck, by whom the children run
Careless with dancing limb,
And laugh, and mock at him;
And beggar, children, towering porch are equal in the sun.

From the opened door bursts upon glorious wings
Music: the shadowy silence moves with sound
That overflows and rolls returning round.
As if to itself, the pillared grandeur sings
Of deeper than all thought has ever found,
Of richer than the heart's imaginings.
Of higher than all hope has dared to see.
Like comment of a crow.
Dulled, reiterate, slow,
The human plaint croaks answer: Vanity! look on me!

Who made the stark unfeatured quarry-block
Live in those song-like pillars? And who smote
The ancient silence into note on note
Melodious as the river from the rock?
Out of the heart of man such splendours float
As make his vileness and his misery mock
The prisoned soul: which shall bespeak him more
Grandeur of stone and sound
Or fawning abject, bound
To his abasement, close as to a dungeon floor?

Sunken eyes, craving hands, defeated shape,
Whom to look on so humbles, you appear
But as the avoided husk, shrivelled and sere.
Cast by the spirit that springs up to escape
To its own reality and radiance there

For ever fresh as young bloom on a grape,
Triumphing to be human, yet to win
An amplitude beyond
Dull care and fancy fond,
And breathe the light that man was born to glory in.

Yet littleness, and envy, and obscure pain
Were mortised into that magnificence!
Trading his wretchedness for pity's pence.
Though this poor ruin from the depth complain,
Slave to his self-lamenting impotence,
Nor can his proud humanity regain;
O Wonder of Man, in his indignity,
Forfeit, disgrace, and rue.
Shares he not still in you?
Did not man sink so low, could he aspire so high?

POEM XLVII

UNSATED MEMORY

Emerging from deep sleep my eyes unseal
To a pursuing strangeness. O to be
Where but a moment past I was, though where
The place, the time I know not, only feel
Far from this banished and so shrunken me,
Struck conscious to the alien dawn's blank peer!

Between two worlds, homeless, I doubt of both.
Knowing only that I seemed possessing realms
And now have nothing. In this glimmering cave
Of daylight, whither I return so loath.
The emptiness of silence overwhelms; —
Still, vision-haunted, like the blind, I crave,

For splendour beats along my blood in gleams
As of a skiey largeness closed and lost,
That memory torments itself to clutch,
Hungering unsated for that light of dreams
Pursued down shadowy paths that foil, exhaust,
And lose me in a cloud I cannot touch.

Fixed as in frost the motionless dim shape
Of each accustomed thing about m}- bed
Is like an enmity at watch for stale
Habit to repossess me past escape.

In the dead light all seems apart and dead.
Yet menaces. The ticked hour is my jail.

Yet I had sense as of a forge whose blast
Could fuse this stark world into glorious flow
Of young power streaming irresistible.
And I, dilated, roamed a region vast.
Feasting in vision, with a soul aglow,
And Time a steed to pace or race at will.

Where is that world that I am fallen from?
Look, as a sea-weed left at ebb to pine
Hueless and shrunken, that had liberty
To wander sparkle-fresh in its own foam,
Trailing its rosy hair in the long brine.
So am I cast up; from what haunted sea?

An ocean of the mind, without access
Save in the labyrinths of sleep, a main
Deep with the memory of all memories.
Thoughts, and imaginations numberless
That ever lodged in the brief-living brain.
Washing our sun lit ignorance: was it this?

Then miserable I, that have but sucked
Dull oozings, vanished into vaporous dew.
From springs that custom closes like a stone
And leaden fear and clayey doubt obstruct.
Heir of the earth's youth and of all it knew,
What am I but a vessel charged with oblivion?

Ah, surely I was rather native there
Where all desires were lovely, and the power
Of Time irrevocably creeping sure
Was uncreated, than in this numb air
Of mapped days and of hour pursuing hour,
Endless impediment and forfeiture.

O we go shrouded from ourselves, and hide
The soul from its own splendour, and encrust
The virgin sense with thinking. Then some chance
Moment reveals us: we are deified.
Feeling and seeing; gold gleams from the rust;
And, marvelling at our lost inheritance.

We breathe the air of beauty; we regale
The mind with innocence; joy has no stint;
And we are chartered for the world's wide sea.

Reason the rudder, not the sky-filled sail. —
Still clings about us some imputing hint
Of strangeness, even in self -captivity.

Before me comes a vision of the old.
With dear experience sunken in their eyes
And furrowed on their faces; scarce a spark
Betrays the quick fire that once made them bold.
All their strength's only for that enterprise
Which takes them soon into the engulphing dark.

I think of old ships stranded, how they stir
The mind to see their beauty in its decay.
For they, unmemoried and mute, have been
Companions of the wild winds without fear.
And carried far adventure, who shall say
Into what glories we have never seen?

POEM XLVIII

THE WOOD'S ENTRY

So old is the wood, so old,
Old as Fear.
Wrinkled roots; great stems; hushed leaves
No sound near.

Shadows retreat into shadow.
Deepening, crossed.
Burning light singles a low leaf, a bough,
Far within, lost.

POEM XLIX

GOBLINS

The night is holy and haunted,
Asleep in a vale of June.
Stillness and earth-smell mingle
With the beams' unearthly boon.—
Yet a terror is fallen upon me
From the other side of the moon.

If it be Truth that's hidden

Upon that other side.
Unseen, unguessed of any,
Waiting to be descried?
Without shadow or footstep.
Goblins by me glide.

The mellow moon, entrancing
An English meadow here,
Silvers the old farm roofs below
And dewy grasses near.
But the world her far side faces?
I think of it, and fear.

If not man's ancient terror.
Bribed with long sacrifice,
If not old ignorance, whose hope
Would truth to itself entice —
If REASON be the goblin
That thrills my blood to ice?

The bean-blossom is breathing
From fields in glimmer spread;
A rose hangs dim on the amber air
But I am lured and led
To an outer vast apartness
Beyond man's hope or dread.

I look down upon me and mine
As with translated eyes,
My struggle in rapture and anguish
But noted like a fly's,
My world at stake, my heaven and hell
Small as a beetle's prize.

Busy in deep-sea dungeoner,
Great mouths of fishes blind;
Blind wheel of planet on planet
In gulfs no thought can find;
The proud black stare of a falcon,
Without a thought behind,

Possess me, dispossess me:
They mock me not, they are.
The worlds are all a web that's hung
Beyond conception far,
That a gorged and hairy spider
Spins in the central star.

Ferocity of begetting;
Prowling hunger's maw.
Fury of teeth and hot-spilt blood.
Cold pounce and tearing claw,
Laughterless lust, the swarm and spawn
That one another gnaw;

A race to death, a frenzy
Rushing into the night,
A rage of life, a riot.
Seen in a moment's light.
And Death the wild pursuer
Close on that fever-flight!

I see it all in vision,
I see with murdered sense
Of neither good nor evil.
Nor make a fool's pretence.
I share, I too, that hunted
And horrible innocence.

Cruelty's matched with courage.
Not that a power should thrive
Which twists its poison- tendrils
In all that is alive;
Nor that with those fell doings
My fate be to connive;

Not this the ulterior terror
That has the goblin grin,
But that the ignorant stare of space
Be the end as the origin, —
This glorious palace of the mind
A cave that tumbles in.
And reason mocked by reason
Be all the goal to win.

POEM L

INITATION

The wind has fal'n asleep; the bough that tost
Is quiet; the warm sun's gone; the wide light
Sinks and is almost lost;
Yet the April day glows on within my mind
Happy as the white buds in the blue air,

A thousand buds that shone on waves of wind.
Now evening leads me wooingly apart.
The young wood draws me down these shelving ways
Deeper, as if it drew me to its heart.

What stills my spirit? What awaits me here?
So motionless the budded hazels spring,
So shadowy and so near!
My feet make not a sound upon this moss, —
Greenest gloom, scented with cold primroses.
A ripple, shy as almost to be mute.
Secretly wanders among further trees;
Else the clear evening brims with loneliness,
With stillness luminous and absolute.

The pause between sun-setting and moonrise
Exhales a strangeness. It melts out in dream
The experience of the wise.
This purity of sharpened sweet spring smells
Comes like a memory lost since it was born.
My own heart changes into mystery!
There is some presence nears through all these spells
Out of the darkened bosom of the earth:
Not I the leaf, but the leaf touches me.

Who seeks me? What shy lover, whose approach
Makes spiritual the white flowers on the thorn?
Who seems to breathe up round me, — perfume strange! —
June and its bloom unborn?
Shy as a virgin passion is the spring!
I could have Time cease now, so there should live
This blossom in the stillness of my heart, —
Earth's earth, yet immaterial as a sense
Enriched to understand, love, hope, forgive.

Now, now, if ever, could the spirit catch.
Beyond the ear's range, thrills of airy sound.
I tremble, as at the lifting of a latch.
Am I not found?
This magical clear moment in the dusk
Is like a crystal dewy-brimming bowl
Imperilled upon lifting hands: I dread
The breathing of the shadow that shall spill
This wonder, and with it my very soul.

A dead bough cracks under my foot. The charm
Breaks; I am I now, in a gloom aware
Of furtive, flitting wing, and hunted eyes.

And furry feet a-scare.
Fear, it is fear exiles us each apart;
We are all bound and prisoned in our fear;
From the dark shadow of our own selves we flee.
Ah, but that moment, open-eyed, erect,
I had stept out of all fear, and was free.

How sweet it was in youth's shy giving-time
Finding the sudden friend, whose thoughts ran out
With yours in natural chime;
Who knew, before speech, what the lips would tell!
No need to excuse, to hide or to defend
From him, in whom your dearest thought shone new
And not a fancy stirred for him in vain.
So was it, as with a so perfect friend.
In that rare moment I have lost again.

But lo, a whiteness risen beyond the hill:
The moon-dawn! A late bird sings somewhere; hark
The long, low, loitering trill!
Like water-drops it falls into the dark.
The earth-sweetness holds me in its fragrant mesh.
Oh, though I know that I am bound afar.
Yet, where the grass is, there I also grew.
Blood knows more than the brain. Am I perhaps
Most true to earth when I seem most untrue?

POEM LI

THE CHILDREN DANCING

Away, sad thoughts, and teasing
Perplexities, away!
Let other blood go freezing,
We will be wise and gay.
For here is all heart-easing.
An ecstasy at play.

The children dancing, dancing.
Light upon happy feet.
Both eye and heart entrancing
Mingle, escape, and meet;
Come joyous-eyed advancing
Or floatingly retreat.

Now slow, now swifter treading

Their paces timed and true,
An instant poised, then threading
A maze of printless clue,
Their motions smoothly wedding
To melody anew,

They sway in chime, and scatter
In looping circles; they
Are Music's airy matter.
And their feet move, the way
The raindrops shine and patter
On tossing flowers in May.

As if those flowers were singing
For joy of the clean air.
As if you saw them springing
To dance the breeze, so fair
The lissom bodies swinging,
So light the flung-back hair.

And through the mind enchanted
A happy river goes
By its own young carol haunted
And bringing where it flows
What all the world has wanted
And who in this world knows?

POEM LII

THE WHARF ON THAMES-SIDE: WINTER DAWN

Day begins; cold and misty on soiled snow
That frost has ridged and crusted. Sound of steps
Comes, then a shape emerges from the mist
Without haste, trudging tracks the feet know well,
With his breath white upon the air before him,
To old work. Over the river hangs a crane
At the wharf's edge. Scarved, wheezing, buttoned up.
The stubble-bearded crane-man eyes the tide
Ruckling against moored barges under the bridge.
Considers the blank moon, the obstinate frost.
Swings arms and beats them on his breast for warmth.
And to his engine-cabin disappears.
Full, fast, impetuous the tide floods up Thames,
And the solitary morning steals abroad
Over a million roofs, intensely still

And distant in a dark sleep.

For whose joy
Was it, the February moon oil night
Beamed silence, like the healing of all noise,
And beauty, like compassion, upon mean
Litter of energy and trading toil, —
Cinder-heaps, sacks, tarpaulins, and stale straw;
Empty and full trucks; rails; and rows of carts,
Shafts tilted backwards; musty railway-arch,
Dingy brick wall, huddled slate roofs? It shone
On the clean snow and the fouled; touches of light
Mysterious as a dreamer's smile! For whom
Rose before dawn the spiritual pale mist,
When imperceptibly the hue of the air
Was altered, and the dwindled beamless moon
Looked like an exiled ghost; till opposite
The vapour flushed to airy rose, and dawn
Made the first long faint shadows?

Now the smoke
Begins to go up from those chimnied roofs
Across the water. Trains with hissing speed
And frosty flashes cross the shaken bridge,
Filled each with faces, eager and uneager.
Tired and fresh, young and old; bound for the desk.
The stool, the counter — threads in the roaring loom
Of London. What thoughts have they in their eyes
That idly fall on the familiar river
This passive moment before toil usurps
Hand and brain? Each a separate-memoried world
Of scheme and fancy, of dreads and urgent hopes.
Hungers and solaces! But which keeps not
A private corner deep in heart or mind
Where dwells what no one else knows? And they pass
Nameless, in thousands, with their mysteries, by us.

Slowly the city is waking in all its streets,
But dark, impetuous, silent, full, up Thames
The tide comes, like a lover to his own;
Comes like a lover, as if it sought to pour
Secrets to its listener, of vast night, and the old
Bright moon-lit oceans; of wild breaths of brine;
Of tall ships that it swung to an anchorage
In the misty dawn, and wanderers far away
On the outer seas among adventurous isles
Whose names are homely here. As if the blood
Of this our race poured back upon its heart,

Drawn by that moon of pale farewell, it comes
Brimming and buoyant, with an eager ripple
Against the black-stemmed barges, and swift swirl
Of sucking eddies by stone piers, and sound
Like laughter along the grimed wall of the wharf.

A great horse, tugging at a truck, stamps hoofs
Upon the frozen ground. A man beside him
Shouts or is silent. Labourers here and there
Deliberately, in habit's motion, take
Each his work: from the barges lighter-men
Call, and the crane moves, rattling in its iron.
It is plain day.

Still the up-streaming tide
Pours its swift secret, and the fading moon
Lingers aloft. But now the wakened wharf,
Stirred from its numbness, the bright rails, the trucks
With snow upon them, and the hoisting crane,
Are touched with all the difference of mankind;
And the river whispering out of the travelled seas
Of foreign ships and countries, comes to them
With a familiar usage; each appears
As a faculty of the morning, that begins
Once more the inter-threaded toil of men.

POEM LIII

THE DREAM HOUSE

Often we talk of the house that we will build
For airier and less jostled days than these
We chafe in, and send Fancy roaming wide
Down western valleys with a choosing eye
To hover upon this nook or on that,
And let the mind, like fingers pressing clay,
Shape and reshape the mould of an old desire.
Spur jogging Time, conjure slow years to days.
Until tall trees, like those far fabled walls.
Rise visibly to the mind's music. Here
We scoop a terrace under hanging woods
Upon the generous slope of a green hill
That gazes over alluring distances;
Listen to our merry children at their play.
And see the shadow lengthen from our roof
On plots of garden. Fancy, busy still.

Sows colours for the seasons in those plots.
And matches or contrasts the chosen leaves
That are to shade our saunters; the clean boughs
Of aromatic walnut; the wild crab
With, after snows of blossom, fiery fruit;
And beeches of a grander race beyond them
Withdrawing into uninvaded wood;
But, farther down, our orchard falls to where
The stream makes a live murmur all day long.
Man is a builder born: not for the shell
That makes him armour against stripping wind
And frost and darkness; for befriending roof
And walls to sally from, a bread-getter.
No, but as out of mere unmeaning sound
And the wild silence he has made himself
Marvellous words and the order of sweet speech,
Breathing and singing syllables, that move
Out of the caverns of his heart like waves
Into the world beyond discovery; so
Builds he, projecting memory and strong hope
And dear and dark experience into stone
And the warm earth he digs in and reshapes,
Dyeing them human, and with a subtle touch
Discovering far kinships in the sky
And the altering season, till the very cloud
Brings its own shadow as to familiar haunts,
And the sun rests as on a place it sought.
Earth also as with a soft step unperceived
Draws from her ancient silence nearer him,
Sending wild birds to nest beneath his eaves
Or to shake songs about him as he walks, —
Shy friends, the airy playmates of his joy.
Caesars may hoist their towers and heave their walls
Into a stark magnificence, impose
The aggrandised image of themselves, as trumpets
Shattering stillness. We'll not envy them.
While there's a garden to companion us
And earth to meet us with her gentle moss
Upon our own walls. They may entertain
Prodigally a thousand guests unpleased;
But we have always one guest that is ever
Lovely and gracious and acceptable,
Light.

As I lay upon a hill-top's turf
I watched the wide light filling the round air
And I was filled with its felicity.
O the carriage of the light among the corn

When the glory of the wind dishevels it!
How it filters into the dim domes of trees
Spilt down their green height, shadows dropping gold!
How beautiful its way upon the hills
At morning and at evening, when the blades
Of grass blow luminous, every little blade!
How the flowers drink it, happy to the roots!
This lovely guest is ours to lodge; and we
Will build for it escapes and entrances
And corners to waylay the early beam
And keep its last of lingering: here to accept
Its royalty of fullness; there to catch
In dusky cool one lustre on the floor
Doubling itself in echoed radiances
Mellow as an old golden wine, on wall
And ceiling: oh, how gentle a touch it has
On choice books, and smooth-burnished wood, in such
Human captivity! When the winds roar over.
What sudden splendours toss into our peace
With reappearing victories! O the glory
Of morning through a doorway on the hair.
Neck, arms, young movements of a laughing child!
O mystery of brightness when we wake
In the night-hush and see upon the blind
The trembling of the shadow of a tree
Kissed by the moon, that from the buried light
Wooes ghostliness of beauty, and receives
And whispers it to all the world asleep.

Whatever it be made of, this dreamed home
Upon a hill, I know not in what vale.
Shall be a little palace for the light
To stray and sleep in and be blest for it.
So thought I: then I thought, O my dear Love,
Surety I am that house, and you the light.

WESTWARD

I found my Love among the fern. She slept.
My shadow stole across her, as I stept
More lightly and slowly, seeing her pillowed so
In the short- turfed and shelving green hollow
Upon a cushion of wild thyme, amid
Tall bracken-tufts that, roughly luminous, hid

Her hair in amber shadow. Then I stopped.
The light was in the West: the wind had dropped;
A burning fragrance breathed out of the ground,
And the sea-murmur rose remote around.
But my Love slept. My very heart was singing
With the sweet swarm of winged thoughts it was bringing:
And she lay there, with the just heaving breast.
So still. As a lark drops down to its nest,
I sank beside her, waiting for those eyes
To complete earth with light that nowhere lies
But in their depths for me, and carry home
The flight of my full spirit.

I had come
From wandering wide beaches far beneath
This airy height of summer-scented heath.
I was alone, and the shore solitary.
And the sea glittered infinite and starry
As on the sands I paced, that dazzling wet
Shone round, until the tumbled rocks they met
At the gaunt cliff's root; silvery runnels, fed
From oozy levels draining to their bed.
Wound flashing between smoothly furrowed slabs
Which the sky coloured; there the youngling crabs
Had scrawled a trail, and weeds, dull-rose and green,
Lay by their shadows, where old foam had been.
Crusted with shells. A mist of finest spray
Blew from the western glory, and in the bay
The ever-streaming surges gleamed and roared
Like a rejoicing Power for ever poured
For the mere splendour of its motion: salt
The air came to the nostril; and the vault
Of heaven had burnt its colours into one
Unfathomable clearness, that the sun
Was soul of, as it journeyed down the West
And in the leaping waters made each crest
A moment of live fire. I breathed the immense
And shining silence. It was to my sense
Like youth, that's all horizon, and misgives
Nothing, and in the unbounded moment lives,
And names not hope yet among things endured
And unamended, being so assured
Of its desire and the long day, and so
Ignorant of that swift Night, saying No.

Ah, why should peace and liberty most bring
Into the heart that loves them most the sting
Of Time's oppression, and the thwarting thorns,

The loss, the want, the many clouded morns?
O for deliverance! To untwist the bond
Of circumstance; to breathe the blest Beyond
Where we would be; to incarnate clean and true
All we were born and dedicated to!
O Love, how often have we shared that sigh!
To me beside that boundless sea and sky
Intolerably came my briefness; all
The undone things. Why into hearts so small
Were crammed these hungering immensities,
Thrust each day back to a prison that denies
Their native satisfaction?

I cast me down
On a great slope of rock that, ribbed and brown,
Was cloven at the top; and in between
The hollowed ledges I could lightly lean
And see the deep cup of a pool; it held
Its limpid leaving of the surge that swelled,
A tide since, over that sea-buried reef.
A round pool, deeply clear beyond belief.
Rough with minute white shells about its rim.
Its crystal in the shadow gleamed how dim
And small! while in my eye the homeless main,
Its brine was of, a splendid restless plain
Of water, spread a path for any keel
To take, the round world over, and to feel
Pressures of every wind, and haven far
Where it should choose, mirroring mast and spar
In sultry smooth lagoon, or under pines
Snow-plumed on iron fiord, or where lines
Of ships at a famed port with traffic hum
And chimes of foreign bells to sailors come.
And strange towers over crowded wharfs look high.
— Ah! such a drop of casual life was I,
At evening left: my simple, scanted, raw
Experience but the sipping of a straw
Snatched from me soon! I lifted up my gaze
Into the west and the spray-misted blaze
Where the sun gloried, and his glittering track
Allured me on and on.

Then I looked back.
All was changed. Something had transfigured each
Of those hard cliffs that thrust into the beach
Their bouldered ramparts. Every narrow seam
Brimmed with the opposite light, and the warm gleam
Found out small clusters of sea-pink, and many

A samphire-tuft in its uneven cranny,
And bloomed a burning orange on the stain
Of lichen, and dissembled rosy grain
On the rock's blackness. At the summit showed
A gemmy green, where the grass patches glowed
Between those jutting crags. The air was hush;
And the shore quivered with a phantom flush
Of molten colours on far-shining sand.
All was as warm to sight as to the hand,
Distinct yet insubstantial, as if what
The eye saw had been created by a thought
Intenser than its vision. Memory played
A music in the mind, and Time delayed
To whisper names forgotten. I saw no more
The sculpture of those rocks, that vivid shore;
But far-off hours arose before me there
Beautiful in a bright unearthly air.
Memory touched her stops, and one by one
They came, each with its own shadow and sun
And its peculiar perfume: each a part
Of the quick blood and pulsing of my heart.
I carried riches; I was as a king,
Clothed in a more than royal apparelling,
Because of glories in the mind, and light
In eyes T knew, and the unended flight
Of thought, and friendship warmer than the sun.
And dateless joy, and hope shared, and things done
With all the soul's strength, and still precious pain.

Youth, O sweet, careless Youth, flooding the vein
With easy blood, what time the body knows
Scarce that it is, so brimmingly life glows
Within it, and its motions are like words
Born happy on the lips, and like the birds
On April-blossomed boughs rich fancies throng
The mind's exuberance and spill in song,
I think my heart back into all the bloom
And feel it fresh. As one that enters home,
I am there: the shyness, and the secret flame
Of ecstasy that knew not any name.
The wild heart-eating fevers, the young tears.
The absorbed soul, the trouble, and the fears
Wide as the night, the joy without a thought
Meeting the morning, — Time has never taught
My heart to lose them. Still I smell that rose
Of so inscrutable sweetness; and still glows
The glory of the wonder when I first
Heard the enchanted poets, and they burst

In song upon my spirit, as if before
No one had ever passed that magic door,
But for me, first in all the world, they sang.
Sweetest of all things. Youth, sweet in the pang
As in the pleasure, you are in me yet.
Changed as the grape to wine: could I forget,
Then were this hand dust. In those yesterdays
Memory happy and familiar strays.
Exploring hours that, long in shadow lain.
Come effortlessly all distinct again.
As in my light boat I would track the banks
Of narrow streams that rippled past the ranks
Of yellow-flowered reeds, and knew not where
They led me, for no human sound was there.
But the shy wings were near me, and I to them.
And the wild earth was round me as in a dream
And I was melted into it. I can hear.
Lost in the green, bright silence, where I steer
Beneath gold shadows wavering on my arm
The water saying over its low charm
Among the reeds, and, dreading to disturb
The mirror of the blossomed willow-herb,
Drink it into my heart. O idle hours.
Floating with motion like the summer towers
Of cloud in the blue noon, I have not drained
Your fullness yet, for all that care has rained
Upon defeated days of dark sundown,
Like burial of all beauty and all renown,
When the spirit sits within its fortalice
And watches mute.

One simple, passionate kiss
Can alter earth for ever. Out of what
Imagination, or what far forethought
Of Time, came Love in beauty new and strange
With eyes of light, my earth and sky to change
And bring me vision of a promised land.
As if long-sunken centuries had planned
The meeting of our lips? From far we came
To one another, ere we had a name.
Wonderful shape, white ecstasy, the cup
That God with living wine has so filled up!
O body made like music, like a word
Syllabled in spontaneous accord;
Quick-sensed with apprehension; capable
Of extreme joy, of pangs far-piercing; full
Of divine wants, like a wave moving through
The passionate and transparent soul of you;

O mystery and power, charged with unknown
Futurities; a lovely flame that's blown
In the wind of life, and sister'd to all fire
That has in it the peril of all desire;
Dearer than breath, what are you made of, whence
Come you? I know not; the eluded sense
Only replies, "To name her is to tell
The very name of Love." It is to spell
A language more profound than tongue can use,
Written in the heart's blood of the world; to lose
All that is worth the losing, and to trust
In spite of withered leaf and charnel dust.

Who knows his own beginning? Hour from hour
Is born; in secret buds, and breaks to flower
Within us. Nothing we have ever been.
Nothing we have endured, nothing we have seen, —
Ay, and before we came into this light,
Were sacrificial hopes, and exquisite
Fears, and the jealous patience of the womb.
And throes of self-consuming martyrdom.
Imprinted on the fibre of our flesh, —
Nothing is ended, but is made afresh
Into a subtler potency; the eyes
See a more wondrous earth, the senses prize
More, its more pregnant meaning; and we go
To enrich a world beyond us, overflow
Into a mind of what thoughts who can tell?

O Love, we draw from an unfathomed well.
Where are the June nights that made heaven a whole
Blue jewel, throbbing through the very soul?
Where is the dizzying bloom and the perfume —
Earth-ecstasy, sighed up to starry gloom.
That in the touching lips' ineffable
Communion, was a spirit and a spell,
As if we had found within ourselves a being
More infinite than any shown to seeing?
Where is the beauty that stole thought away
And moved to tears some one remembered day?
Where is the laughter some sweet chance would start,
To leave its summer warmth about the heart?
Where are the places we shall see no more?
Are they not powers to haunt us at the core
Of feeling, and evoke the eternal Now,
Like music, out of nothing? Nay, I vow,
Most perishable, most immortal tastes;
And the frail flame, that touches us and hastes

Into the dark, endures more than the build
Of proudest fortress. We are found and filled;
And it suffices. For we pass among
Grandeurs, and from a grandeur we are sprung.
Marvellous in our destiny, and know
Man is most man meeting a giant foe.
Whether overcoming or defeated. We,
Who hear, like moving rumour of the sea
And march of ocean waves, the human sound
About us, filled with meaning more profound;
Who know what hearts beat by us, and have shared
In all the mighty martyr names have dared;
Who feel all earth beneath the stars, the race
Of rivers, and the mountains in their place,
Faculties of our being; and have a mind
Dyed in the ardent story of our kind;
We in our briefness, in our storm and ache,
Our loves magnificent in hearts that break.
We, all our bonds and bounds (xceeding, ay.
Burning a loftier flame because we die,
We at Time's outpost, we the thrust spear-head
Against the opposing darkness of the dead,
We are the world's adventure! We speed on.
Stay not, but westward travel with the sun,
Westward into the splendour that takes all.
And carry far into the great light's fall
That infinite memory of the world we bear
Within our spirits, burning and aware.

Wake, Love, awake! — Her eyes shone into mine
That moment. In the air was light divine,
Sinking and yet suspended still, to hold
Rocks, ocean, heaven, within one bath of gold.
But in the soul that met me from those eyes.
Impassioning the beauty of the skies.
Was my completion. Earth as newly made,
Ev'n to the smallest shape of green grass-blade,
Lived; and the thrilled, bright silence sang to me;
For in the hush I heard the boundless sea.

POEM LV

FROM THE CHINESE

A flower, or the ghost of a flower!
Mist, or the soul of it, felt

In the secret night's mid hour.
Lost on the morning air!
Who shall recover it, — ^beauty born to melt
As the apparition of blossom brief and shy,
As the cloud in the sky that vanishes, who knows where?

POEM LVI

THE COCKATOO: FROM THE CHINESE

A present from tropical Annam,
A bird with a human speech,
A gloriously plumed cockatoo
Rosy as the flower of a peach!
And they did what they also do
To the learned, the witty, the sage; —
Got a cage with the stoutest of bars
And shut it up fast in the cage.

POEM LVII

FROM GOETHE

Peace is perfect over
All the hills.
Scarce wilt thou discover
A breath, so still's
Every tree.
The woods are silent; birds have hushed their song.
Wait but thou; ere long
Peace comes to thee.

POEM LVIII

IN MEMORY OF GEORGE CALDERON

Wisdom and Valour, Faith,
Justice, — the lofty names
Of virtue's quest and prize, —
What is each but a cold wraith
Until it lives in a man
And looks thro' a man's eyes?

On Chivalry as I muse.
The spirit so high and clear
It cannot soil with aught
It meets of foul misuse;
It turns wherever burns
The flame of a brave thought;

And wheresoever the moan
Of the helpless and betrayed
Calls, from near or far.
It replies as to its own
Need, and is armed and goes
Straight to its sure pole-star; —

No legendary knight
Renowned in an ancient cause
I warm my thought upon.
There comes to the mind's sight
One whom I knew, whose hand
Grasped mine: George Calderon.

Him now as of old I see
Carrying his head with an air
Courteous and virile,
With the charm of a nature free,
Daring, resourceful, prompt,
In his frank and witty smile.

By Oxford towers and streams
Who shone among us all
In body and brain so bold?
Who shaped so firm his themes
Crystal-hard in debate?
And who hid a heart less cold?

Lover of strange tongues,
Whether in snowy Russia,
Or tropic island bowers
Listening to the songs
Of the soft-eyed islanders.
Crowned with Tahitian flowers,

A maker of friends he went.
Yet who divined him wholly
Or his secret chivalries? —
Was all that accomplishment.
Wit, alertness, grace.

But a kind of blithe disguise?

Restless in curious thought
And subtle exploring mind,
He mixt his modern vein
With a strain remotely brought
From an older blood than ours,
Proud loyalties of Spain.

Was it the soul of a sword?
For a bright sword leapt from sheath
Upon that August day
When war's full thunder stored
Over Europe, suddenly crashed,
And a choice upon each man lay.

Others had left their youth
In the taming years; and some
Doubted; some made moan.
To meet the peril of truth
With aught but a gay courage
Was not for Calderon.

Wounded from France he came.
His spirit halted not:
In that long battle afar.
Fruitless in all but fame,
Athos and Ida saw
Where sank his gallant star.

O well could I set my mood
To a mournful falling measure
For a friend dear and dead;
And well could memory brood
Singing of youth's delight
And lost adventure fled.

But that so fearless friend
With his victorious smile
My mourning mood has chid.
He went to the very end;
He counted not the cost;
What he believed, he did.

POEM LIX

I

Victory! Was that proud word once so dear?
Are difficulty, patience, effort hard
As danger's edge, disputing yard by yard
The adversary without and the mind's fear.
Are these our only angels? friends austere
That find our hidden greatness out, and guard
From the weak hour's betrayal faith unmarred!
For look! how we seem fall'n from what we were.

Worms feed upon the bodies of the brave
Who bled for us: but we bewildered see
Viler worms gnaw the things they died to save.
Old clouds of doubt and weariness oppress.
Happy the dead, we cry, not now to be
In the day of this dissolving littleness!

II

O you dear Dead, pardon! For not resigned.
We see, though humbled, half our purpose bent
And our hope blurred, like men in banishment.
Giants amid a blank mist groping blind,
The nations ache. And old greeds unconfined
Possess men, sick at battle's blood hot-spent
Yet sleek and busy and righteously content
To wage war, safe and secret, on their kind.

If all were simple as the way of hate!
But we must reap where others sowed the seed
In time long past, of folly and pride and greed;
Confused with names, idols, and polities;
Though over all earth, where we think a State,
There are but men and women; only these.

III

Victory, winged, has flown far off again.
She is in the soul, she travels with the light.
We see her on the distant mountain height
Desired, but she has left us in the plain.
Left us awhile, to chafe and to complain.
Yet keep our wills, in this dark time's despite.

Like those that went up to the horrible fight
Beneath their burdens, plodding in the rain.

Courage! The same stuff that so greatly bore
And greatly did, is here, for gods to find.
And the dear human cause in the heart's core.
Be the task always harder than we know.
And victory further, yet in pain we grow.
The vision is before us, not behind.

POEM LX

A DAFFODIL

Pure-throated Flower,
Smelling of Spring,
Shaped beyond art's
Imagining;

Fathomless colour,
Breathed as an ether
Of flame and of stillness
Melted together;

Soul of the sun's beam
Changed to fairy
Flesh, so delicate,
Poised and airy!

I think of my own kind,
Hardly winning
A thousand battles
For joy's beginning;

Victory bloody
And with evil shared,
Splendour soiled
And greatness snared;

Truth conceded
Or won by halves,
Pitiful sores
And sorrier salves;

Blind authority
Treading like oxen's heels

All that sees clearest.
All that most feels.

But you are absolute
(Follow who can!)
As a commandment
Of God to man.

Straight you spring
And whole you spend,
And fall upon fruitful earth.
Clean to the end.

O to be pure
As a single sense,
Keen as scorn,
As love intense,

To live in the light,
And to die in a deed
That is faith's Amen
And has sown its seed!

Laurence Binyon – A Short Biography

Robert Laurence Binyon, CH, was born on August 10th, 1869 in Lancaster in Lancashire, England to Quaker parents, Frederick Binyon and Mary Dockray.

He studied at St Paul's School, London before enrolling at Trinity College, Oxford, to read classics.

Binyon's first published work was Persephone in 1890. Whilst only a few pages in length it certainly illustrated the talents that Binyon would develop as a poet even though he continued to advance multiple career opportunities.

Immediately after graduating in 1893, Binyon started work at the British Museum for the Department of Printed Books, writing catalogues for the museum and art monographs for himself. As well as being one of England's best poets he was also renowned for his knowledge of various arts particularly with regard to Japan and Persia.

His first poetry book Lyric Poems was published in 1894.

In 1895 his first art book, Dutch Etchers of the Seventeenth Century, was published and, that same year, Binyon moved into the Museum's Department of Prints and Drawings.

Whilst Binyon became known to a wide audience as a poet his output was not prodigious. In 1898, Porphyrion & Other Poems was published followed by Odes (1901) and The Death of Adam & Other Poems (1904).

That same year, 1904, Binyon married the historian Cicely Margaret Powell. The union was to produce three daughters.

In the early years of the 20th Century Binyon was a regular patron of the Wiener Cafe of London together with fellow artists and intellectuals; Ezra Pound, Sir William Rothenstein, Walter Sickert, Charles Ricketts, Lucien Pissarro and Edmund Dulac.

His poetic work continued despite the demands of the British Museum and his other interests. London Visions was published in 1908 followed by England & Other Poems in 1909.

His work at the British Museum ensured promotions were a frequent occurrence for Binyon. In 1909, he became its Assistant Keeper, and in 1913 he was made the Keeper of the new Sub-Department of Oriental Prints and Drawings.

It was also at this time that he played a crucial role in the formation of Modernism in London by introducing young Imagist poets such as Ezra Pound, Richard Aldington and H.D. (Hilda Doolittle) to East Asian visual art and literature.

Many of Binyon's books produced while at the Museum were influenced by his own sensibilities as a poet, although some are clearly works of plain scholarship, such as his four volume catalogue of all the Museum's English drawings, and his seminal catalogue of Chinese and Japanese prints.

Binyon's poetic reputation before the war, although built on several slim volumes, was such that, on the death of the Poet Laureate Alfred Austin in 1913, Binyon was among the names considered as his likely successor. It was quite a field. Among the other illustrious contenders were Thomas Hardy, John Masefield and Rudyard Kipling; however the post was awarded to Robert Bridges.

Moved and shaken by the onset of the World War I and its military tactics of young men slaughtered to hold or gain a few yards of shell-shocked mud as the British Expeditionary Force began its campaign Binyon wrote his seminal poem For the Fallen, with its Ode of Remembrance (the third and fourth or simply the fourth stanza of the poem). The poem was published by The Times newspaper on September 21st, when public feeling was shaken by the recent Battle of Marne. It became an instant classic, turning moments of great loss into a National and human tribute.

Today, For the Fallen, is often recited at Remembrance Sunday services as well as being an integral part of Anzac Day services in Australia and New Zealand and of November 11th Remembrance Day services in Canada. The "Ode of Remembrance" is now acknowledged as a tribute to all casualties of war, irrespective of nation.

In 1915, despite being too old to enlist, Binyon volunteered at a British hospital for French soldiers, the Hôpital Temporaire d'Arc-en-Barrois, Haute-Marne, France, working for a short time as a hospital orderly.

He returned there in the summer of 1916 and took care of soldiers taken in from the Verdun battlefield. He wrote about his experiences in For Dauntless France (1918) and his poems, "Fetching the Wounded" and "The Distant Guns", were inspired by his hospital service.

After the war, he returned to the British Museum and wrote numerous books on art; especially on William Blake, Persian and Japanese art. His work on ancient Japanese and Chinese cultures offered inspiration that inspired many, among them the poets Ezra Pound and W. B. Yeats. His work on Blake and his followers kept alive the then nearly-forgotten memory of the work of Samuel Palmer. Binyon's spectrum of interests continued the traditional interest of British visionary Romanticism in the rich strangeness of Mediterranean and Oriental cultures.

In 1931, his two volume Collected Poems appeared and by 1932, Binyon was promoted to the post of Keeper of the Prints and Drawings Department. The following year, 1933, he retired from the British Museum. He went to live in the country at Westridge Green, near Streatley but continued writing poetry.

In 1933–1934, Binyon was appointed Norton Professor of Poetry at Harvard University. He delivered a series of lectures on The Spirit of Man in Asian Art, which were published in 1935.

Binyon continued his academic work: in May, 1939 he gave the prestigious Romanes Lecture in Oxford on Art and Freedom, and in 1940 he was appointed the Byron Professor of English Literature at the University of Athens. He worked there until forced to leave by the German invasion of Greece in April, 1941.

Binyon had been friends with Ezra Pound for a long time, and in the 1930s the two became especially close; Pound affectionately called him "BinBin", and he assisted Binyon with his translation of Dante.

Between 1933 and 1943, Binyon published his acclaimed translation of Dante's Divine Comedy in an English version of terza rima, made with some editorial assistance by Ezra Pound. It was acknowledged for many decades as *the* popular translation for Dante readers.

During the horrors of the Second World War Binyon wrote a poem that many claim as to be a masterpiece 'The Burning of the Leaves', puts in print his lines on the London Blitz.

At his death Binyon was working on a major three-part Arthurian trilogy, the first part of which was published after his death as The Madness of Merlin (1947).

Robert Laurence Binyon died in Dunedin Nursing Home, Bath Road, Reading, on March 10th, 1943 after undergoing an operation. A funeral service was held at Trinity College Chapel, Oxford, on March 13th, 1943.

Binyon's ashes were scattered at St. Mary's Church, Aldworth.

On November 11th, 1985, Binyon was among sixteen poets of the Great War commemorated on a slate stone unveiled in Westminster Abbey's Poets' Corner. The inscription on the stone quotes a fellow Great War poet, Wilfred Owen. It reads: "My subject is War, and the pity of War. The Poetry is in the pity."

Poems and Verse
Persephone (1890)
Lyric Poems (1894)
The Praise of Life (1896)
Porphyrion & Other Poems (1898)
Odes (1901)
Death of Adam & Other Poems (1904)
Penthesilea (1905)
London Visions (1908)
England & Other Poems (1909)
Auguries (1913)
For The Fallen (The Times, September 21st, 1914)
The Winnowing Fan (1914)
The Anvil (1916)
The Cause (1917)
The New World: Poems (1918)
The Secret: Sixty Poems (1920)
The Idols (1928)
Collected Poems Vol I: London Visions, Narrative Poems, Translations (1931)
Collected Poems Vol II: Lyrical Poems (1931)
The North Star & Other Poems (1941)
The Burning of the Leaves & Other Poems (1944)
The Madness of Merlin (1947)

Poems Set to Music
In 1915 Cyril Rootham set "For the Fallen" for chorus and orchestra, first performed in 1919 by the Cambridge University Musical Society conducted by the composer.

Edward Elgar set to music "The Fourth of August", "To Women", and "For the Fallen", as The Spirit of England, Op. 80, for tenor or soprano solo, chorus and orchestra (1917).

English Arts and Myth
Dutch Etchers of the Seventeenth Century (1895), Binyon's first book on painting
John Crone and John Sell Cotman (1897)
William Blake: Being all his Woodcuts Photographically Reproduced in Facsimile (1902)
English Poetry in its relation to painting and the other arts (1918)
Drawings and Engravings of William Blake (1922)
Arthur: A Tragedy (1923)
The Followers of William Blake (1925)
The Engraved Designs of William Blake (1926)
Landscape in English Art and Poetry (1931)
English Watercolours (1933)
Gerard Hopkins and his influence (1939)

Art and freedom. (The Romanes lecture, delivered 25 May 1939). Oxford: The Clarendon press, (1939)

Japanese and Persian Arts
Painting in the Far East (1908)
Japanese Art (1909)
Flight of the Dragon (1911)
The Court Painters of the Grand Moguls (1921)
Japanese Colour Prints (1923)
The Poems of Nizami (1928) (Translation)
Persian Miniature Painting (1933)
The Spirit of Man in Asian Art (1936)
Autobiography[edit]
For Dauntless France (1918) (War memoir)

Biography
Botticelli (1913)
Akbar (1932)

Stage Plays
Brief Candles A verse-drama about the decision of Richard III to dispatch his two nephews
Paris and Œnone. A Tragedy in One Act (1906)
Godstow Nunnery: Play
Boadicea; A Play in eight Scenes
Attila: A Tragedy in Four Acts (1907)
Ayuli: A Play in three Acts and an Epilogue
Sophro the Wise: A Play for Children
(Most of the above were written for John Masefield's theatre).

www.ingramcontent.com/pod-product-compliance
Lightning Source LLC
Chambersburg PA
CBHW060050050426
42448CB00011B/2383